The Soldier

THE CIVIL WAR SOLDIER AT ATLANTA

By Carl R. Green and William R. Sanford

Illustrations by George Martin

Edited by Jean Eggenschwiler
and Kate Nelson

PUBLISHED BY

Capstone Press

Mankato, MN, U.S.A.

Distributed By
⊄P CHILDRENS PRESS®
CHICAGO

CIP

LIBRARY OF CONGRESS CATALOGING IN PUBLICATION DATA

Sanford, William R. (William Reynolds), 1927-
The Civil War soldier at Atlanta / by William R. Sanford, Carl R.
Green.
p. cm.-- (The Soldier)
Summary: Recreates the experience of one soldier in theCivil War
as he fights with William T. Sherman in theBattle of Atlanta.
1. Atlanta, Battle of, 1864--Juvenile literature. 2. United States.
Army--History--War of 1864--Juvenile literature. [1.Atlanta, Battle
of, 1864. 2. United States--History--War of 1864--Campaigns.] I.
Green, Carl R. II. Title. III. Series: Sanford, William R. (William
Reynolds), 1927- Soldier.
E717.1.S22 1989
973.8'9--dc20   **89-25136 CIP AC**

Illustrated by George Martin
Designed by Nathan Y. Jarvis & Associates, Inc.

Pub 2/92 11.95

Capstone Press

Box 669, Mankato, MN, U.S.A. 56001

CONTENTS

AN IOWA FARMER FIGHTS FOR THE UNION

From 1861 to 1865, the United States was caught up in a terrible civil war. It was a war that matched the armies of the South against those of the North. By the time the fighting ended, four out of every ten soldiers were dead or wounded. The nation had suffered over a million casualties.

The people of the North fought for two great causes. First, they were determined to preserve the **Union**. Second, they wanted to free the black slaves. The people of the South answered that the Federal government was trampling on their rights. They had to fight, they said, to protect their way of life.

The names of Civil War generals are

featured in American history texts. For the North, Generals Ulysses S. Grant and William T. Sherman stand out. The Southern generals, especially Robert E. Lee and "Stonewall" Jackson, were just as capable. These generals earned most of the medals, but the common soldier made the war possible. Armies are made up of enlisted men who fight—and often die—for what they believe is right.

Justin Cook was one of those ordinary Americans. He was born on a farm in Langworthy, Jones County, Iowa. As a boy, he quit school early to help work the family land. It was a hard life but a good one. Justin married Katherine Hartman in 1859 and built her a house on land he had homesteaded. Katherine was expecting their first child when the Civil War started.

Many Northerners said the war would be over in six months. Justin did not think so. He knew that the Southerners would be fighting for their homes and families. In August of 1862 he enlisted for three years in Company H, 31st Infantry, Iowa Volunteers. He was just 26 years old, and fit from his work in the fields. Katherine cried and told him it was not his war to fight. Justin hugged

Atlanta, Georgia, and the surrounding battle area.

her and tried to explain. "Like Mr. Lincoln says, we can't live half slave and half free," he told her.

Justin took his basic training at Davenport, Iowa. From there, the 31st traveled by Mississippi River steamboat to Arkansas. In the months that followed, Justin saw service at the battles of Vicksburg, Missionary Ridge, and Lookout Mountain. In 1864, as part of General Sherman's army, he headed deep into Georgia. If the army could take Atlanta, the victory would deal the South a serious blow.

SHERMAN HEADS FOR ATLANTA

Sergeant Justin Cook led his platoon down a dirt road. The swirling dust filled his nose and made him sneeze.

"If we aren't slogging through mud, we're choking on red Georgia dust," he complained. "It's been two months since we headed south out of Tennessee behind old Billy Sherman. But my knapsack isn't getting any lighter." He slapped at a fly.

"Cheer up, Sarge," Corporal Sam Wingate called. "We'll catch **Johnny Reb** one of these days. When we do, we'll whip him."

Like many others, Sam thought the campaign would be over as soon as Sherman destroyed the Rebel army. Justin was not as sure. It did not look as though they were ever going to force the Rebels into a fight to the finish.

Justin and his platoon belonged to General William Tecumseh Sherman's Army of the Tennessee. Sherman also commanded the Army of the Ohio and the Army of the Cumberland. The three armies had marched into Georgia in early May, 1864. By mid-June, the 100,000 men had covered almost a hundred miles. The rutted road led through a wild country of steep gorges, swollen rivers, and thick forests. In country like that, Sherman could not depend on slow-moving supply wagons. He ordered each man to carry extra supplies in his knapsack. Justin had heard they were saving at least 300 wagons.

As platoon sergeant, Justin had checked the men's equipment that morning. Their knapsacks were stuffed with mess gear, clothing, and personal items. In addition, each man carried a bed roll, half of a two-man tent, ammunition, a rifle, and a canvas **haversack**. The haversack held three days' food rations. Just now, the rations were mostly salt pork, coffee, sugar, salt, and tasteless **hardtack** crackers.

Each night the men spread out and stripped the land of whatever food they could find. Sherman approved of the practice. "War is cruelty," he said. "There's no use trying to reform it. The crueler it is, the sooner it will be over."

It was Sam's turn to cook. He was making stew from crushed hardtack, water, and greens. "Say, Sarge," he said, "besides tiring us out, what is Uncle Billy Sherman aiming to do?"

Justin was cleaning his rifle. "We're here to smash Joe Johnston's army and tear up Georgia," he said. "If we keep the Rebels busy, they won't be able to send any help to General Lee up in Virginia. President Lincoln will surely thank us for that."

Day by day, Sherman pushed forward. By the middle of May, the fighting had heated up. A **Confederate** force stopped Sherman's advance near the town of Resaca. The Yankees responded by sending an army around Joe Johnston's flank. The Rebel general had to retreat or risk being surrounded. He chose to pull back. His goals were to keep his army together and to give up land slowly.

On June 27 Sherman failed to drive the Southern defenders from Kennesaw Mountain. Patiently, he returned to his flanking actions. Johnston withdrew to the Chattahoochee River. When Justin stood beside the river three days later, he was only ten miles from Atlanta. The Union army found a gap in the Southern defenses and forced its way across the river. Once he had enough men across, Sherman launched another **flanking attack**. This time Johnston was forced to fall back to the city's defenses.

Justin was ready to go on guard duty that night when a friend from Company B grabbed his arm. "The boys found this Atlanta newspaper," the sergeant said. "It admits that Grant's moving on Richmond, and that we're almost to Atlanta. But that's not all. The Rebel president, Jeff Davis, thinks Johnston is afraid to fight. He's fired ol' Joe and given command here to John Hood."

"Isn't Hood the general with only one leg?" Justin asked. "I heard they have to strap him into his saddle when he rides."

"Yeah, he has a bad arm, too," the sergeant said. "But he's young, only 34, and he's a gambler. He'll hit us hard."

Justin nodded. "Sherman will like that," he said. "He's dying to fight on open ground."

The sergeant smiled. "He can handle Hood," he said.

"Some of the Northern papers say that Sherman's crazy," Justin reminded his friend. "They've been down on him ever since he wouldn't let their reporters into Chattanooga. And there are people up North who don't like the way he uses the Tennessee railroads to carry our supplies. They think the trains should be carrying food for Reb civilians. Those editors should ask how we feel. The 31st Iowa likes Sherman just fine."

"With Hood against Sherman," the sergeant said with a smile, "we're in for a real fight!"

CAMP LIFE DURING
THE SIEGE OF ATLANTA

"Army life is full of 'hurry up and wait'," Justin wrote to his wife. The platoon was resting after a long, hard march. Justin knew that new orders might come tonight—or next week.

"Your last letter took three weeks to reach me," he continued. "That's about average for mail delivery. I thank you for news of the baby and the farm."

Not far away, smoke rose from a burning cornfield. "Our men destroy the crops we don't need," he wrote. "Unless the war ends soon, this state will be a wilderness." Because no one censored his letters, Justin was free to write whatever he wanted.

"It's turned warm, so I no longer sleep in a tent," he wrote in his strong, slanting hand. "I roll up in blankets and hope it doesn't rain. Most of all I wish I had some soap. We're all crawling with lice, and there's no way to get rid of them."

He paused and chewed on his pen for a moment. "Still, we're better off than the Confederates," he went on. "Some are still fighting like tigers. Others are ready to give up. Yesterday most of their **skirmish line** came over to our side. They were barefooted, and their uniforms were in tatters."

Justin tried to answer a question from Katherine's last letter. "You asked me how the army is organized. Well, as you know, our 31st Regiment is part of the Army of the Tennessee. The army is divided into corps, divisions, and brigades. The 31st is one of five regiments in our brigade. My platoon belongs to C Company of the 31st Regiment.

"I'd better stop now because I have to clean my rifle. Captain Peabody gives us extra duty if our weapons are dirty."

Justin inspected his muzzle-loading **Springfield rifle**. The gun was a fine weapon—simple, rugged, and accurate. It weighed almost nine pounds and was about 56 inches long. When a soldier received his rifle, he also signed for an 18-inch **bayonet** and scabbard, a cap box, and a cartridge box. Like the other Yankee soldiers, he wore all of these on his belt.

Loading a Springfield was only a little faster than loading an old flintlock rifle. First, Justin took a paper cartridge from his case. He tore one end with his teeth and dumped the powder down the barrel. Then he pressed the bullet into the barrel and jammed it home with a ramrod. After snapping the ramrod back into place, he pulled the hammer back to

16

half cock. Now he took a percussion cap and fitted it into place. Setting the hammer back to full cock was the final step. When he pulled the trigger, the hammer snapped down on the cap. The hot gases produced by the exploding cap set off the powder in the barrel, firing the rifle.

Captain Peabody called on Justin whenever he needed a sharpshooter. The Iowa farmer could hit a bull's-eye at 300 yards. The Springfield had a range of 1,000 yards, but its accuracy was poor at that distance. The rate of fire was slow, as with any muzzle-loading rifle. At his best, Justin could get off only three shots a minute.

While he loaded, Justin longed for one of the new **Henry repeating rifles**. A few units had them, but not the 31st. The Henry held 15 rounds and could be fired as quickly as a man could work its lever action. Justin had offered a soldier $20 for his Henry, but the man only laughed. As the Rebels said, a Henry could be loaded on Sunday and fired all week.

The sound of a train whistle reminded Justin that the 31st was due for railroad duty. The railroad was Sherman's lifeline, and he kept it well protected. The main threat was from Confederate cavalry units. These swift horsemen could tear out miles of track before the Yankees knew they were there. And sometimes bands of Southern civilians sneaked in to burn a bridge or derail a supply train.

The army had brought in 2,000 civilians to lay track and to rebuild bridges. "I wouldn't trade places with those fellows, even if they do make $2.00 a day," Justin told Sam. "They're easy targets for Rebel snipers, and they can't fight back."

After one tour of guard duty Justin started another letter. "It was amazing," he wrote. "The Railway Construction Corps built a new bridge over the Chattahoochee. It was 800 feet long and nearly 100 feet high. They had to start by chopping down trees for the timbers. But they did the job in under five days! Seeing the trains steaming right up to the camp was a real boost for our morale.

"The railroads may be the key to beating Johnny Reb," he continued. "Atlanta is the last major rail center in the deep South. If they lose the city, the Confederates will have a hard time moving men and supplies.

"With love to my little family,

JUSTIN"

FREEDMEN, PRISONERS, AND POLITICS

Long lines of former slaves followed Sherman's army as it moved deeper into the South. Most of the refugees were confused by the war and by their new freedom. Change had come too fast. Drifting behind the army, hundreds died from hunger and disease.

The army set up camps for the **freedmen** and their families. The small, crowded camps needed guards, but the regular soldiers hated this duty. "I didn't join up to be a policeman," Justin complained in one of his letters. He felt better after some freedmen were given uniforms and trained as camp guards.

Since 1863, the Union had been

organizing army units made up of black men. Most were used as laborers, but a few battalions were sent into battle and they fought well. Sherman was not interested in adding black regiments to his command. He did not mind using the freedmen as laborers, however. Each division commander was allowed to hire up to 200 blacks for $10 a month per man. The workers dug trenches and built fortifications while the regular troops slept. The pay did not seem low to Justin. He made only $20 a month himself, and privates earned just $16.

Like most Northerners, Justin had joined up to preserve the Union. In addition, he believed that the slaves should be freed. The more he talked to the freedmen the more he saw them as worthwhile human beings. Some of the men called the blacks **"contraband."** Contraband was Southern property that the army had a right to seize. Justin knew that freeing slaves hurt the South, but he did not like to think of human beings as property.

When he bossed a black work gang, Justin told the men about the **Emancipation Proclamation**. "It was Mr. Lincoln who set you free," he said. The freedmen agreed that Lincoln was a brave man and a great President.

Justin received a sad letter one evening. Katherine's brother had been taken prisoner by the Rebels. Justin knew that some soldiers joked about surrendering. "At least you won't get shot in a prison camp," they said. Only fools took such talk seriously. Life in a "Johnny Reb hotel" was no joking matter.

Katherine wrote, "I hope and pray that Louis will be exchanged." Justin knew better. During the first years of the war, the two sides had exchanged prisoners. A general, for example, had been worth 60 privates. The exchanges stopped after Grant took command in 1863. Captain Peabody had explained the general's thinking. "The South is running short of men," he said. "Prisoner exchanges build up their armies and lengthen the war."

Did Louis have a chance of surviving prison life? Justin knew that military prisons were bad. The Rebel prison at Andersonville, Georgia, was the worst. Prisoners died every day of **dysentery**, typhoid, infections, and poor food. Medical care was almost never available.

When Justin asked Captain Peabody about the prisons, the captain shrugged. "No one really planned it this way," he said. "Modern war is brutal beyond belief. The South can barely feed its own people, let alone thousands of prisoners."

The soldiers argued politics all that summer. Lincoln was running for reelection as the Republican candidate. He had picked Andrew Johnson, an anti-slavery Democrat, as his running mate. The Democrats had nominated General George McClellan.

As usual, Sam Wingate jumped into the argument with both feet. "If I were president," he said, "I'd lock up all of those

Peace Democrats. They call themselves Copperheads because they wear Indian heads cut from pennies on their lapels. I call 'em Copperheads, too—the poisonous snakes!"

"Sam, you and General Burnside think alike," Justin said with a laugh. "Last year, Burnside put Congressman Vallandigham in jail for siding with the Rebs. He stayed there, too, until Lincoln shipped him south to make trouble for Jeff Davis."

The November election was not far off. Justin knew that a vote for Lincoln would be a vote to continue the war. A vote for McClellan would be a vote for ending the war on terms favorable to the South.

"We've got attacks pressing hard against Richmond and Atlanta," Justin told Sam. "One of them better produce some results right quick. Otherwise, the country will elect a peace president. Why, the Democrats even let Vallandigham return from the South to make the keynote speech at their convention. If they win, all of our fighting will have been for nothing."

THE REBELS BUILD
STRONG DEFENSES

Now that they were across the Chattahoochie River, Atlanta lay within reach. Justin told his platoon that Hood was certain to take the offensive.

The Rebels were not their only worry. Digging trenches in the July heat left the men soaked with sweat. At night they were eaten alive by hungry mosquitoes. Justin longed to exchange his heavy winter uniform for summer clothing. He might as well have wished for the moon. Ammunition and food came before uniforms when supply trains were being loaded.

The date was July 18. As usual, Justin had slept in his cotton flannel "drawers." When he rolled out of his blanket, he quickly pulled on a wool shirt and light-blue trousers. Next came a dark-blue jacket, buckled at the waist by a black leather belt. His rough black shoes (the men called them "gunboats") had worn large holes in his socks. Finally Justin ran his fingers through his long hair and put on his blue cap. He was lucky. Because he was of average build, his clothes fit fairly well.

The thought of breakfast reminded Justin that he felt a little sick to his stomach. Serves me right, he thought. Last night he had eaten too much hardtack fried in pork fat. It was a dish known as "skillygalee". But he could smell the smoked hams that had been "liberated" by a **foraging** party. Justin cut a big chunk of ham and washed it down with hot coffee. To his relief, his stomach stayed calm. As he ate, he dreamed of big platters of fresh vegetables. Army-issue split peas and dried potatoes tasted like old boots.

Captain Peabody took Justin on an inspection tour of the regiment's trench lines. Whenever the army stopped, Sherman ordered them to dig in. It was slow going, but digging cut down on casualties. The Rebels were doing the same thing. Army scouts had seen 50 miles of trenches around Atlanta.

Peabody said they would soon make another flanking movement. Justin smiled, knowing it would drive the Confederates crazy.

As he followed the captain, Justin admired the work of the **sappers**. These hard-working engineers saved lives with their shovels and axes. He and the captain walked past dug-in artillery batteries and ammunition bunkers. Next came the parallel rows of reinforced trenches. Each was connected to the others by narrower zigzag trenches.

The troops on the front line lived in dugout rooms known as bombproofs. When they were on duty, they watched the enemy's movements from behind a headlog. This was a heavy timber that was raised up a few inches on support beams. The headlogs also protected the riflemen when they were firing.

As Justin and Peabody entered the forward trench, a soldier saluted. "The **pickets** are bringing in a prisoner," he told Peabody. A minute later, a dirty, bearded Southerner tumbled into the trench. His head was bleeding where he had been clubbed by a Yankee rifle butt. Peabody asked him about the Rebel defenses.

"Sherman can attack forever, and we'll

just go on killing Yankees," the man said proudly. "We've been setting up defenses for a year now. Our slaves have chopped down thousands of trees to give Hood's cannon a clear field of fire. The defenses are laid out in squares, about three miles on a side. They're reinforced with barriers of logs and pointed stakes."

"How strong are your trenches?" Justin asked the man.

The Rebel looked around. "If you attack, we'll show you some real trenches," he said. "Your infantry will be going up against walls made of strong timbers. Our riflemen will pick you off like quail! The trenches are reinforced with logs and sandbags. Even a direct hit from an artillery shell won't collapse them."

The prisoner's words had the ring of truth. Justin knew how difficult it was to assault those positions. Less than a month ago, at Kennesaw Mountain, Rebel rifle fire had killed six men from his own company.

"You can't win," Captain Peabody told the prisoner. "We outnumber you and we'll outfight you."

The Rebel raised his bloody head and glared at Peabody. "General Hood has three veteran corps," he snapped. "And he's expecting more troops from Virginia. While you yellow-bellied Yankees are sitting around, Hood will pick his spot. Then he'll smash you."

Peabody told the soldiers to take the man away. He turned to Justin. "He's wrong, Sergeant. Sherman is too smart for the Rebels. He won't make a frontal attack. He'll cut the rail lines that feed the city, and Hood will have to retreat. Mark my words, we'll walk into Atlanta free and easy."

THE BATTLE OF
ATLANTA BEGINS

"We've cut the Georgia railroad! It's on to Atlanta!" The young lieutenant yelled and waved as he spurred his horse past Justin's regiment. No one moved. The day was too hot.

It was noon on July 19, a steamy Tuesday. Justin's platoon had just torn apart a small wooden house to make a shade roof. The shade helped a little, but not much.

The 31st had been hard at work all morning. As part of General McPherson's Army of the Tennessee, they were swinging in from the east toward Atlanta. Their job was to cut the Georgia Railroad near Decatur, six miles east of the city. Without the railroad,

Hood would not be able to get fresh troops from Virginia by train.

The men had been ripping up rails all morning. Justin and his company stacked the ties and set them afire. The men then threw sections of track onto the blazing fires. When the rails glowed red-hot, they were lifted with tongs and wrapped around the nearest trees. Once they cooled, they would be there forever.

As the afternoon wore on, Justin helped bend one last rail. "There's another of Uncle Billy's bow ties," he told Sam. "But it's too quiet. I can't believe Hood isn't going to fight."

"From what I hear, our three armies are too spread out," Sam replied. "Hood is smart enough to see that. He might try to hold us and the Army of the Ohio with a small part of his forces. Then he could throw everything else against General Thomas and the Army of the Cumberland."

Justin nodded. "I hope Thomas stays alert," he said.

Sam turned out to be a good prophet. On Wednesday, July 20, they heard the sound of heavy firing to the west. Was Thomas in trouble? Justin's platoon came running when a dispatch rider rode into camp and dropped down from his sweaty horse. An officer ran up and grabbed his reports. When the rider asked for something to drink, Sam handed him a tin cup filled with coffee.

"The Army of the Cumberland was almost across Peachtree Creek by four o'clock," the man said. "We had seven divisions spread out on a front that was about three miles wide. I was up on a ridge a little south of the creek. All at once we heard the Rebel yell and the Johnnies were attacking.

"Did Thomas let them catch you spread out on both sides of the creek?" Justin demanded.

"Of course not," the soldier said angrily. "The army was mostly across. Pap Thomas, he was still on the north side of the creek when the Rebels opened up. That did not stop him. His horse artillery sent Hood's boys diving for cover. By then more of our divisions were in position to fight. Luckily, the Confederates never sent in their reserves. They finally broke off the fight and pulled back toward Atlanta. We think Hood's saving his reserves to block your army's advance along the railroad."

The Army of the Tennessee was now within artillery range of Atlanta. That same

Wednesday afternoon, Justin watched as the batteries fired their first 20 shells into the city. Hood's attack at Peachtree Creek had cost him 3,000 men and gained him nothing. Atlanta was still under **siege**.

On Friday, July 22, a new rumor swept through the regiment. It looked as though Hood was withdrawing from Atlanta! The men on the advance skirmish line had brought back the news that morning. The Rebels seemed to be leaving their positions on the north and east of the city.

The celebration did not last long. Hood was not a quitter. The Rebel general had guessed that McPherson was heading south to cut the city's last rail line. Hood put together a plan aimed at crushing the exposed left flank of the Union army. He ordered General Hardee's four divisions to hit the Union flank from the east. A second force under General Cheatham was held back, ready to attack from the west.

Justin heard the first rifle fire just after midday. Hardee's men surged forward, only to run into a Union corps of 5,000 men under General Dodge. The Yankees wheeled left and formed a defensive line. Backed by artillery, they stopped the first Rebel charge. For hours the fighting seesawed back and forth. The Union line bent but refused to break. In the confusion of the battle the men saw McPherson's horse running loose. A little later they found the general's body.

The 31st was dug in on the right flank. At about three o'clock Justin heard the shrill Rebel yell. "They're coming!" he shouted, and sighted on a Confederate officer. Before he could fire, a bullet punched through his left arm. He spun around, stumbled, and fell. He felt as if he had been kicked by a mule.

THE REBELS ABANDON ATLANTA

The air above the Yankee line seemed to be full of Rebel bullets. As Justin held his bleeding arm, Sam crawled over to him. The corporal ripped off a piece of his own shirttail and tied it tightly above the wound. "Move off the battle line," he said as he knelt to reload. "A man could get killed up here."

Justin joined a group of walking wounded. They climbed to higher ground and looked down on the battlefield. The Union line was bent into an L-shape. To the south, Hardee's Rebel attack seemed to be running out of steam. The real danger was building on the west side of the line.

As he stood there, Justin's arm started

to throb and his knees felt weak. He sat down and leaned against a tree. Not far away he saw General Sherman and his staff. They were watching their men being pushed back in vicious hand-to-hand fighting. Slowly a gap was opening in the Union lines.

"Use your artillery!" Justin muttered. Sherman seemed to hear him. The general ordered every cannon in the Army of the Ohio into action. When the barrage began, he called for a counterattack from the north. General Logan, who had replaced McPherson, mounted a drive that closed the gap in half an hour.

The afternoon wore on. Twice the Confederates attacked the center point of the L. Each time, the Union troops met them head-on and threw them back. As darkness fell, Hardee's battered Rebels withdrew into the woods. Hood lost more men in five days than Joe Johnston, the man he replaced, had lost in ten weeks.

Justin found a supply wagon which was serving as an ambulance. The driver took him to the division hospital. A young surgeon cut the bullet from his arm and bandaged the wound.

"You're lucky, Sergeant," he said. "No

broken bones and a clean wound. Do you want something for the pain?"

"Save it for the boys who are badly hurt," Justin said, shaking his head. Medicines were always in short supply.

A second wagon took Justin back to his unit. He found the men huddled around a tiny fire. "Sam caught a bullet in the throat," Private Turner said. "He's dead, along with Wilder." Justin was numb from the shock of his own wound. "Another good man dead," he said quietly. "We're going to miss Sam."

The next few days were quiet. The pain of Sam's death hit hardest when they buried him. Justin wept for his friend and then went back to work. His wound was starting to heal. Three new men arrived to join the platoon. Justin showed them a map of Atlanta. "Uncle Billy's too smart to try a frontal assault on the city," he said. "He's going to try to cut the Rebs' last rail line." He pointed to a spot southwest of the city.

On July 27 the Army of the Tennessee set off to circle the city from the north. As he studied his compass, Justin saw that they were swinging down to the southwest. Their long march ended at a country chapel called Ezra Church.

The men quickly built a defense line from fence posts and logs. Then they waited. Hood sent two divisions against them the next day. The Yankee line held through a day of bloody fighting. When it was over, Hood had lost another 5,000 men.

But a defensive victory was not enough for the North. The last railroad was still in Rebel hands. Captain Peabody told Justin that Sherman was sending one cavalry force to tear up the tracks. Another was ordered to liberate the Union prisoners at Andersonville. The two raiding parties bagged a few Rebels but failed to complete their missions.

Whichever way Sherman moved, Hood seemed to be there before him. "The enemy can build defenses faster than we can march," he wrote to General Thomas. Angry and frustrated, Sherman turned his artillery on the city. On a single day, 5,000 shells rained down on Atlanta.

The Union army's new trenches were inching toward the Rebel lines. Justin slept during the day and dug at night. It was at night that the two armies sometimes called a brief, unofficial truce. Soldiers met between the battle lines and traded Yankee coffee for Rebel tobacco. One night Justin's company sang "Battle Hymn of the Republic" for the Confederates. The Rebels answered with a chorus of "Dixie."

Sherman took a bold gamble aimed at ending the siege. First he sent his wagons, baggage, and surplus troops back to the Chattahoochee. Then, on August 25, he moved south. Five days later, the Union army reached the last Rebel railroad. The men destroyed the tracks and easily beat off Hood's counterattack.

Justin watched the ties burning and smiled. Sherman's army had the Rebels almost encircled. Hood knew it, too. On September 1 the earth shook as his men blew up the guns and powder they could not carry with them. Then they retreated. On September 2, Yankee troops entered the city. The Battle of Atlanta was over.

AFTER THE BATTLE

On September 2, 1864, Sherman sent a telegram to Washington. It ended with the words, "So Atlanta is ours, and fairly won." That message changed the course of the Civil War.

If the Confederates had won at Atlanta, the South might be a separate nation today. Hood gambled that he could beat Sherman by leaving his defenses and going on the attack. As a result, he lost 20,000 men and the city of Atlanta. He also lost the 1864 election and what remained of the war.

The Battle of Atlanta was fought at a time when the North was almost worn out. The **casualty** lists were long, and victory seemed far away. The Democrats were

promising to make peace if they were elected. The news from Atlanta drove away some of the gloom. In November 1864, Northern voters reelected President Lincoln. The South's last hopes vanished at the same time.

But the Confederates did not give up. The Union army had more work to do. For one thing, Hood's army was still dangerous. Sherman sent General Thomas' army in pursuit. Then Sherman took 60,000 men and headed for the Atlantic coast at Savannah. The "March to the Sea" cut a fiery 60-mile-wide path across Georgia. The soldiers burned bridges, warehouses, factories, and barns. The men feasted on fresh beef, pork, eggs, fruit, and vegetables. A crowd of good-for-nothings called "bummers" trailed behind, stealing whatever was left. As Sherman said, this was "war with the lid off."

Justin's regiment marched proudly into Savannah on December 22. Sherman sent a wire to Lincoln, offering the city as a Christmas gift. That night Justin and his platoon dined on oyster stew and roast goose. After burning much of the state, the army left Savannah untouched when it moved north in February.

The war ended two months later. The 31st was camped in North Carolina when Lee surrendered to Grant on April 9, 1865, in Virginia. After all the fighting and suffering, the Civil War was over.

Justin was released from the service in

November. He put on civilian clothes and caught a train back to Iowa. His wife and young son welcomed him. Katherine gave him the sad news about Louis dying in the prison at Andersonville.

Two days later Justin was out mending fences and planning the spring planting. He picked up a handful of black Iowa soil and smiled. It felt good to be home again.

GLOSSARY

Important Historic Figures

JEFFERSON DAVIS (1808-1889)—President of the Confederate States of America during the Civil War.

GENERAL ULYSSES S. GRANT (1822-1885)—Commanding general of the Union forces during the Civil War. Grant later became the 18th President of the United States.

GENERAL JOHN BELL HOOD (1831-1879)—Brave, gambling Confederate general who lost the Battle of Atlanta.

GENERAL JOSEPH JOHNSTON (1807-1891)—Confederate general whose defensive tactics displeased Jefferson Davis. Davis replaced Johnston with Hood shortly before the Battle of Atlanta.

GENERAL ROBERT E. LEE (1802-1870)—The Confederacy's most successful general during the Civil War.

ABRAHAM LINCOLN (1809-1865)—The leader and inspiration for the North during the Civil War. Lincoln was the 16th President of the United States. He was assassinated less than a week after Lee surrendered in April 1865.

GENERAL WILLIAM TECUMSEH SHERMAN (1820-1891)—Union general who fought and won the Battle of Atlanta. Sherman understood the horror and brutality of war.

Important Terms

BAYONET—A knife that fits on the muzzle end of a rifle. Soldiers use bayonets in hand-to-hand combat.

CASUALTY—Someone who is killed or wounded in a military action.

CONFEDERATE—A common name for the Southern rebels who tried to withdraw from the Union.

CONTRABAND—Enemy goods or property that may be seized during wartime.

DYSENTERY—An infection of the lower intestines that causes pain, fever, and diarrhea.

EMANCIPATION PROCLAMATION—A proclamation issued by President Lincoln on September 22, 1862 that freed the Confederacy's slaves.

FLANKING ATTACK—A strategy by which an army tries to hit an opposing force on one on its unprotected sides.

FORAGING—Soldiers going into the country-side to take whatever food they can find.

FREEDMEN—Former slaves who were freed by the Emancipation Proclamation.

HARDTACK—Hard, unsalted crackers that were an important part of a soldier's diet during the Civil War.

HAVERSACK—A canvas sack in which Union soldiers kept their supply of food.

HENRY REPEATING RIFLE—A Civil War rifle that could fire 15 shots before it had to be reloaded.

JOHNNY REB—A slang name for Confederate soldiers.

PICKETS—Soldiers sent out on guard duty to protect a camp from an enemy attack.

SAPPERS—Soldiers whose main job is that of constructing fortifications.

SIEGE—The attempt to capture a city by surrounding it and forcing its defenders to surrender.

SKIRMISH LINE—A group of soldiers who go out ahead of the main body of troops to probe the enemy's defenses.

SPRINGFIELD RIFLE—The muzzle-loading rifle used by most of the Union troops during the Civil War.

UNION—A common name for the states that fought against the Confederacy.